The Little Book of Modern Magic

Incantations and Practices to Create Magic in your World

*A Channeled Text
By Rachael L Thompson*

Disclaimer

This text is intended for entertainment purposes only. Everything expressed in the book is the author's personal opinion and should be viewed as such. Results are not guaranteed.

The author and publisher do not assume and hereby disclaim any liability to any party for any loss, damage, or disruption caused by readers' use of the information. Personal judgment and discernment are always recommended while reading this text.

This book is not intended as a substitute for the medical advice of professionals. The reader should regularly consult a physician in matters relating to his/her physical and mental health, particularly concerning any symptoms that may require diagnosis or medical attention.

Copyright © 2020 by Rachael Lynn Thompson
All rights reserved. This book or any portion thereof
may not be reproduced or used in any manner whatsoever
without the express written permission of the publisher
except for the use of brief quotations in a book review.

Table of Contents

Read First: Introduction — 1

Part One: Magical Rituals & Practices — 5

Ritual Suggestions — 6
Cleansing, Clearing, and Protection — 7
Full Moon Ritual — 9
New Moon Ritual — 10
Candle Magic — 11
Water Magic — 12
Crystal Magic — 15
Releasing Ritual — 17
Manifestation Ritual — 18
14 Archangels to Assist in Practice — 19
Gods, Goddesses, Ascended Masters and Deities to Assist in Practice — 21

Part Two: Spells, Incantations, and Activations — 25

Introduction — 26

Love and Relationship Spells — 29

Spell 1: Attract New Relationship — 30
Spell 2: Call in SoulMate or Twin Flame — 31
Spell 3: Heal Relationship — 32
Spell 4: Cutting Cords — 33
Spell 5: Improve Communication — 35

Self Healing and Empowerment — 37

Spell 6: Release Fear and Doubt — 38
Spell 7: Self Love and Confidence — 39
Spell 8: Step into Personal Power — 41
Spell 9: Peace and Tranquility — 42
Spell 10: Physical or Mental Healing — 43

Bonus Spell: Healthy Weight or Ideal Body Type   44
Bonus Spell: Anti-Aging or Reverse Aging Spell   45

Unlock Magic Within   47

Spell 11: Unlock Unique Gifts Spell   48
Spell 12: Violet Flame Invocation Spell   49
Spell 13: Uncover Life Purpose Spell   50
Spell 14: Spiritual Downloads Spell   51
Spell 15: Connect with Angels or Spirit Guides   52

Success and Abundance Spells   53

Spell 16: Money Spell   54
Spell 17: Manifestation Spell   56
Spell 18: Success Spell   57
Spell 19: Clear All Financial Blocks   58
Spell 20: Career or Business Spell   59

Releasing Spells   61

Spell 21: Release Old Attachments   62
Spell 22: Dissolve Blocks   64
Spell 23: Forgiveness Spell   65
Spell 24: Release Old Relationships   66
Spell 25: Release All Unwanted Energy   67

Spiritual Expansion Spells   69

Spell 26: Heart Opening Spell   70
Spell 27: Chakra Balancing Spell   71
Spell 28: Align with Source Spell   74
Spell 29: Transcend Ego Spell   75
Spell 30: Open Third Eye Intuition Spell   76

Advanced Spells — 77

Spell 31: Attunement Spell — 78
Spell 32: Ancestral Healing Spell — 79
Spell 33: Open Akashic Records Spell — 80

The End. The New Beginning. — 81

About the Author — 82
Additional Resources: Where to Connect with Rachael — 83
Resources and Favorite Things — 83

Read First: Introduction

Modern-day spells, incantations, and activations for all intentions.

This is a simple, yet powerful intention setting book. All incantations are channeled and infused with high vibrational energy. By repeating the incantation you unlock the energy placed into each word.

Every incantation can be used as many times as you need, each working with your specific intentions and needs at that time. Angels and other Divine Light Beings were called upon during the creation of the incantations. Each word is also infused with Reiki Energy and the alchemy powers of the Violet Flame.

This book is intended for quality over quantity. You will find some suggestions on how to use these incantations, but it is always best to follow your guidance on how to utilize the power of the written words.

NOTE-All incantations are infused with energy that can only be used for the highest and best good. The power within this book is spiritually protected and cannot be used for ill-will, negative intentions, or to cause harm to self or others in any way.

The incantations are tools to assist in your personal energetic, spiritual, healing, or magic practices. They do not originate from any particular spiritual or energetic origin. They hold magic unto themselves and can be used in conjunction with other tools or on their own.

You are a creator. These incantations assist in your creation process. May all words be spoken with the purest of intentions, as part of Divine Will, and for the highest and best good of all involved. May all self-imposed limitations, obstacles, blocks, and limiting beliefs be transmuted into light. May all energy from fear, anger, resentment, grief, and pain be transmuted into love, peace, and sovereign power.

You are Divine. You are Light. You are Love. May your radiance shine for all to see. May your unique gifts and powers manifest to their fullest potential. May you be free from lower vibrational energy and fully embrace your highest spiritual and human potential. May you know your worthiness and deservingness of all the blessings your heart desires. May you feel your Oneness with All that is. May you always feel love for yourself and the Oneness that we all share. With much love and gratitude. So mote it be. It is done. We give thanks.

Part One:
Magical Rituals & Practices

Ritual Suggestions

The suggestions in 'Part One' of this book can help enhance the incantations. These are basic guidelines and can be modified to your needs. Get creative. It is highly suggested that you do a brief cleansing and protection process before any ritual or incantation. See the basic guidelines in the next section.

The various practices described are not based in any particular spiritual practice. They were designed to be simple, requiring zero base knowledge and limited materials. This is purposeful. If you have been practicing rituals for some time, you may skip this section as the incantations hold the true power.

Cleansing, Clearing, and Protection

It is always wise to do any ritual or incantation from a clear space, both internally and externally. We all carry energy with us and often external energy can attach to objects, rooms, or people. This is not to say the outside energy is 'bad' but when doing magic it is always wise to start with a clean energetic slate. You can use these practices on their own or in conjunction with your rituals or spells.

Clear Your Space

1. Smoke is an excellent way to clear your space. Sage is the most commonly used tool and can be bought at any metaphysical store or farmers market. Palo Santo comes from a sacred tree in South America and is said to not only clear but also infused with space with sacred energy. Smoke from incense can also be used but is debatably less powerful than sage or palo santo. Another option is a selenite crystal. This is the only crystal that does not need cleansing and can be used to cleanse yourself, space, and other crystals.
2. Walk around your space with your preferred clearing agent, making sure to get in all the corners of the room. As you are walking around your space, state 'I cleanse with space of all energy that is not of love and light.'
3. Draw 3 figure eights or infinity symbols in the middle of the room using your smoke or crystal.
4. Open windows to let all old energy out or ask that all energy is neutralized and transmuted into pure divine light energy.

Clear Your Personal Energy Field

Using one of the suggested tools listed above, wave smoke or crystal around the entire body. Outline the body from head to toe and then run the cleansing tool over the front and back of the body. State personal intention for clearing and cleansing the mind, body, and aura.

Cleansing Objects

Using cleansing tools listed above, wave the object through the smoke stating 'May the smoke cleanse this object of any old, impure, or residual energies.'

Protection

There are various ways to protect yourself and your space. Listed below are a few. Use them individually or in combination.

1. Visualize a white light surrounding you and the room. Set the intention you and your space are protected by this Divine Energy and only love and light may enter the space.
2. Call in your guides and angels to protect you and the space. Archangel Michael provides strong, protective energy when called upon, but you may call on any guide, deity, or angel you feel drawn towards.
3. Place crystals around you or your space. Place four protective crystals, such as obsidian, hematite, black tourmaline, or smokey quartz, around you or in the corners of your room. Ask that the crystals protect you and your space.
4. Place salt around you. You can draw a circle of salt around you, or for a less messy option, pour salt in little bowls and place four bowls of salt around you or your space, creating a protective barrier.

Full Moon Ritual

Traditionally Full Moons are a time for great release as well as fruition of previous intentions. The moon holds great power and energy that can enhance your personal magic. Simply laying under the full moon and talking to Goddess Luna opens the door to incredible clarity.

Full moons are a great time to set your crystals outside to cleanse and charge. You can also set a jar of distilled water in the moonlight and drink it the next day to embody the power of the moon. Journaling, meditating, and taking a relaxing bath during a full moon are all simple full moon practices.

Pick an incantation that resonates and state it 3 times asking Goddess Luna to bless your words with her wisdom.

New Moon Ritual

New Moons are traditionally a time for manifestations. It is a good practice to set an intention during each new moon cycle. Stating the intention aloud, visualizing it, or writing it down will add power, as they all add elements of energy.

If you can, sit outside or by a window as you write down your intentions. Call in the power of the new moon and ask Her to bless these intentions. State them aloud, slowly while feeling the energy of the words. As you fall asleep that evening, hold the paper with your intentions at your heart chakra and visualize the fruition of your dreams. Place the paper under your pillow and sleep with it under there until the next new moon. You can also sleep with it under your pillow for 3 nights and then place the paper on an altar or next to your bed with a crystal on top.

Candle Magic

Materials

- Candles
- Candle Holder
- Sage, Palo Santo, or Selenite Crystal
- Salt or Protection Stones
- Pencil or Toothpick

Ritual

1. Purchase Candles. Candles designed for magic can be purchased at your local metaphysical store. You can also buy any stick candle you desire, and create magic using your intentions.
2. Cleanse room and candles using sage, palo santo, or selenite crystal. See the 'Cleansing' Section for details.
3. Hold the candle with your left hand and place the right hand over top. State your intention for this candle.
4. You may also carve your intention into the candle using a pencil or toothpick.
5. Place the candle in a holder and surround it with salt or protection crystals.
6. Light candle.
7. As the candle burns, repeat intention or incantation as many times as you desire.
8. Allow the candle to burn down.
9. Meditate on the intention with palms turned up as candle burns.
10. If a candle is too big to burn in one setting, continue to light the same candle while stating the incantation for 3-7 days past the initial ritual.

Water Magic

Water is an incredibly powerful agent and carrier for intentions and energy. Studies done by Dr. Masaru Emoto showed how words affect the crystalline structure of the water. In his experiments, he found that positive words or intentions create beautiful crystals after the water is frozen, while negative words create distorted structures.

Dr. Emoto's experiments gave scientific validity to what humans have been doing for centuries. Holy water, used by the Catholic church, is the most well-known spiritual use of water for healing and protection, but it's also something humans use innately without realizing it. Think of how many vacationers travel to water, beach or lake, to relax. Or when we are trying to de-stress, we take a bubble bath. Some people cannot start their day without taking a shower first. Although these all seem like normal human activities, there is a deeper reason we are so drawn to water to help us feel better.

Water is a blank slate. It is a Divine gift for us to use how we choose. It is mutable and will carry the intentions we place into it. It works as a cleansing agent, as well as a carrier for new intentions. Our bodies are made of approximately 60 percent water, with our heart and brain being composed of 73 percent water. It is also free and widely available. Water may be one of the most underutilized tools for transformation and magic. When used intentionally, it can help shift your inner and outer world in infinite ways. Below are seven ways to use water magic. You can use these practices with any of the incantations listed in this book.

1. *Water Cleansing.*
   Take a bath or shower with the intention of cleansing or releasing all that no longer serves you. If taking a showing, state aloud what you are releasing as you wash your body. Focus on areas where you feel physical tension. If taking a bath, state everything you choose to release into the water. Ask that the water washes away all that no longer serves you. Adding in Epsom salt or a salt scrub can aid in this process. When you are complete with your bath or shower, watch as

all the water drains from the tub. Envision that it takes all your worries and old energy with it.

2. *Water Manifestation.*
Fill a cup with water. On this cup write or state the current situation you want to shift. Write your manifestations or incantation on a new, empty cup. Pour the water from your current cup to the new cup. Allow the intentions to infuse the water for a minute or two. Drink the water and feel yourself leaping into this new reality.

3. *Daily Shower Magic.*
You can do magic each time you take a shower. When you are washing your body, state a releasing incantation or specifically say what you wish to release. After the cleansing, set the intention of what you want to call into your being, peace, love, abundance, etc. Ask the energy of your intentions to infuse the water. As the water washes over you, open yourself up to receive this new energy.

4. *Ocean Spell for A New Beginning.*
If you have the privilege of being by an ocean, you can harness its enormous power for your personal intentions. Ask the Goddess of the Ocean for her Divine assistance in your process. And make sure to give gratitude for her help.
For clarity on your next steps, walk along the shore, right where the ocean comes to wash away your footprints. State your intention to move on from your current situation into a new one. Ask for clarity and whatever else you need to step forward into a new chapter. Watch as the water washes away your footprints and creates a blank slate for you to create anew.

5. *Moon Water.*
Place a jar of distilled or spring water outside during the full moon. Write or state intentions to be infused in the water. You can also place crystals in the water for extra power. Allow water to sit out under a full moon overnight. The next evening, state your desired incantation and drink the water. If using crystals, sleep with them under your pillow for 3-7 nights.

6. *Water Bottle Magic.*

   This is another simple practice you can do daily. Any time you pour yourself a glass of water, set the intention you are infusing in this water. If you have a bottle or cup you can write on, write affirmations to infuse the water. You can also state an intention while holding a water-safe crystal and place it within your water bottle. It just takes a second to state a simple blessing over any food or drink item. It's a subtle habit that can create amazing results over time.

7. *Water Alchemy.*

   Alchemy is the process of transmuting one energy into another. Everything is energy and energy cannot be destroyed. Energy is constantly changing forms and you can use water to intentionally shift any lower vibration energy into whatever you desire.

   To start your water alchemy process, simply write on one side of a piece of paper everything you wish to transform. On the opposite side of the paper, write what you intend to transmute the unwanted energy into. For example, you would write lack on side one and abundance on side two, confusion on side one and clarity on side two, or loneliness on side one and loving companionship on side two. Once you are finished, place paper in a jar of water. Ask the water to please transmute all old energies into your intentions. Allow the water to sit for 1-3 days. This is also excellent to do on a New or Full moon. Once you feel the transmutation has occurred, dump the water out into the earth. Ask Mother Earth to take this new energy and grow physical manifestations of your intentions. Give thanks to the water and Mother Earth for assisting you.

Crystal Magic

There are limitless ways to incorporate crystals into any magical practice. Crystals carry their own unique power that can be enhanced with your personal use of them. They magnify any intention you set and can be cleansed and recharged anytime you desire. Crystals can be used as a part of a ritual or simply carried around for added metaphysical support during your day. They help you and your space stay in a high vibrational state. Below are 7 ways to incorporate crystals into any ritual or practice.

1. *Infuse crystals with your intention.*
   While holding a crystal in your left hand, hover your right hand over top while stating an intention or incantation. Once the words are spoken, swipe right hand three times over the crystal, sealing in the energy.

2. *Hold crystals to amplify intention or incantation.*
   While speaking intention aloud, hold the crystals you feel will best amplify this energy. Ask crystals to help send energy into the ether and ground it within you.

3. *Crystal Grid.*
   Write your intention on a piece of paper. Place crystals over that will help amplify the energy. For a simple crystal grid, place one main stone in the center of the grid. This would be the stone you believe embodies the powers of the intention the greatest. Place four clear quartz crystals around the center stone to amplify it further. Finally, you can place additional crystals in each corner of the paper.

4. *Crystal Meditations.*
   While laying down, place crystals on parts of your body you feel need healing or clearing. You can also place a stone at each of the seven main chakra centers or localized chakra points, such as the heart or third eye. Holding one clear stone, used for higher frequencies, and one dark stone, used for grounding energies, can create an incredible energetic cycle throughout your body.

5. *Crystals under a pillow.*

   Infusing a crystal with an intention and then sleeping with it under your pillow for 3-7 nights can create incredible healing while you sleep.

6. *Crystal Water.*

   Putting crystal in drinking water creates a simple, modern-day potion. Place crystals in a jar of distilled water and place outside during the full moon. State intention and leave outside the entire night. Drink water and sleep with crystals under your pillow for 3-7 nights after.

   Take a crystal bath by adding crystals and essential oils to bathwater. State intention while drawing bath water or repeat incantation while in the bath.

   Finally, you can add crystals to your everyday drinking water. They even make crystal water bottles.

   Note: Not all crystals can be added safely to water. Also, Epsom salt may deteriorate some stones. A quick online search will help ensure you and your crystals stay safe.

7. *Tarot and Crystal Magic*

   Most people think of tarot or oracle cards as divination tools used for guidance. But they can also be used for magic. You can deliberately choose a card whose message resonates or pull a card for guidance.

   Once you select a card, ask that the elements of this card are either called into or released from your life. Then choose a crystal to place over it for 3-7 days to assist in this process. Place a card and crystal next to your bed or on your altar, if you have one. Allow the tools to work their magic on your behalf. Remember to give them gratitude daily for their work.

Releasing Ritual

There is nothing as freeing as a good energy release. Whether you need an energetic release from a recent situation or a deep cleansing from years of programming and limiting beliefs, this ritual can be catered to any intention.

To begin, grab a journal or a few pieces of paper.

Write: *I release everything written below, from the point of its creation, and all residual energy that has taken form since. I release this from within me and from my outside world now and forever. So be it and so it is. Thank you.*

Next free write, listing everything you wish to release. Allow this to pour out of your subconscious mind and Soul without any censorship. Write until you feel the emptiness of all the energy within.

Optional: Read aloud what you have written to solidify the process.

Safely burn the paper. If burning is not an option, tear it up and throw it away in a disposal area outside of your living space.

After you have disposed of the paper, get a shower to finalize the releasing process. Grab a white washcloth and salt rub. While in the shower, imagine you are completely cleansing all last bits of the energy from you permanently. Once this process feels complete, towel off and meditate for at least 5 minutes, setting new intentions moving forward.

Be gentle with yourself after such an intense ritual. It may take a while for the energy to fully settle so it is best you do this when you do not have anything to do afterward.

Manifestation Ritual

The most important point to remember while trying to manifest is what you are trying to manifest is You. At the core, everything is energy and we are all connected in the Unified Field of Energy. There is no separation between you and what you desire. The only apparent separation comes from the misperception of the ego. It can be a hard concept to wrap our minds around because it is not meant to be understood on a cognitive, or mental, level. Open yourself up to Oneness and allow the Universe to show you proof of the Law of Creation. It always will when you are open to it.

With this in mind, how you choose to manifest it is completely up to you. Since the early 20th century, teachers have shared concepts on the Law of Attraction, each sharing unique viewpoints with supporting evidence for their effectiveness. Some suggestions included visualizing intentions, writing or 'scripting', and speaking affirmations. All work. What creates change is how much each strategy shifts your energy into the vibrational match of your intended manifestation.

To create is Divine. It does not matter if we create with our minds, voice, or hands, the energy of creation is ever-present. Once you realize you are a Divine Creator, you will not need rituals or practices. But until the embodiment of this knowledge, it can be helpful to find a strategy that helps you Know your manifestation is unfolding.

Steps to Manifest Using Incantations

1. Take a few very deep breaths. Imagine you are inhaling fresh, cleansing energy and exhaling all old, stagnant energy.
2. Set the intention you are open and ready to receive.
3. Write or visualize your intention, as if you are currently experiencing it.
4. State your chosen incantation
5. Imagine the energy from the incantation is merging with the energy from your intention
6. Imagine all of that energy merges with your being.
7. You are now One with this energy. And so it is.

14 Archangels to Assist in Practice

Archangel Ariel- Manifestation, Healing, Peaceful Power, Connection between Physical and Metaphysical

Archangel Azrael- Transformation, Death and Rebirth, Addictions, Mediumship, Helps Souls Cross Over, Comfort from Grief or Loss

Archangel Chamuel- Inner Peace, Unconditional Love, Self Love, Relationship Harmony, Physical Health and Weight Loss, Finding Lost Items

Archangel Gabriel- Help with Career or Business, Creative Pursuits, Life Purpose, Sacral Chakra Healing, Nurturing, Children, Fertility, Inner Child Healing

Archangel Jeremiel- Emotional Healing, Forgiveness, Healing from Trauma, Grief, Shadow Work, Guidance, Clarity on Life Lessons Being Learned

Archangel Jophiel- Helps Clear Internal or External Clutter, Energy Clearing, Beauty, Balance, Clarity, Access to Higher Knowledge, Distinguish Between Ego and Higher Self

Archangel Metatron- Crown Chakra Opening, Intuition, Higher Knowing, Connection to Divine, Spiritual Connection, Spiritual Healing, Healing Karma, Energy Work, Divine Guidance, Release Worries, Clear Lower Energies

Archangel Michael- Protection, Cutting Cords, Releasing Attachments, Grounding and Root Chakra Healing, Security, Safety, Strength, Perseverance, Power

Archangel Raguel- Communication, Relationship Healing, Friendship, Cheer and Happiness, Peace and Harmony, Fairness

Archangel Raphael- Healing, Assist Healers, Miracles, Support, Physical and Emotional Health, Heart Chakra, Planetary Healing, Access to New or Ancient Healing Techniques

Archangel Raziel- Psychic Abilities, Metaphysical Practices, High-Level Understanding, Unlock Spiritual Gifts, Discover Soul's Purpose, Understanding Dreams and Synchronicities

Archangel Sandalphon- Divine Messages, Prayer, Affirmations, Intentions, Music, Clarification, Truth, Power Through Words, Carries Your Message to Others

Archangel Uriel- Divine Light, Meditation, Clarity, Higher Perspective, Clear Mind of Confusion, Decision Making, Brainstorming New Ideas, Solutions

Archangel Zadkiel- Learning, Forgiveness, Compassion, Love, Reconnection, Life Purpose, Discernment, Divine Intervention, Healing Relationships Through Love, Freedom, Alchemy, Justice

Gods, Goddesses, Ascended Masters and Deities to Assist in Practice

A deity is an aspect of the Divine. Each carries particular traits of the One Divine Creator and can assist when needing help in a particular area of your life. There are many Divine Helpers spoken about in various religions and spiritual belief systems. Some were human, often revered as Saints or Masters, while others are aspects of the Divine who have not incarnated in human form.

It is strongly recommended you do further research before calling on a particular Being. There are many more than listed in this section. This is an abbreviated list I created from my experience (those whom I worked with). If you are unsure who is best for you to work with, ask the question, and it will be answered by the Universe.

You will find they all carry a different energy. You can call on them by asking for their help by name. You can also mantra their name, repeating their name over and over until you feel their energy within your field. You can also repeat specific mantras that are associated with them while calling upon their energy. Some traditions suggest an offering, such as fruit or flowers, in exchange for their assistance. Always be sure to give your gratitude for their help along your journey.

List of Gods, Goddesses, Ascended Masters and Deities

Divine Mother- Feminine Aspect of Divine, Unconditional Love, Compassion, Comfort, Creation, Acceptance, Flow, Allowing, Overcoming Barriers through Surrender

Divine Father- Masculine Aspect of the Divine, Knowledge, Guidance, Action, Accomplishing Goals, Life Purpose, Overcoming Barriers through Force

Jesus- Ascended Master, Unconditional Love, Compassion, Oneness, Enlightenment

Buddha- Ascended Master, Spiritual Evolution, Overcoming Illusions, Compassion, Growth, Enlightenment, Freedom from Ego

Saint Francis of Assisi- Peace, Healing, Animals, Nature, Environment

Saint Germain- Master of the Violet Flame, Spiritual Alchemy

Lakshmi (Hindu Feminine Deity)- Good Fortune, Abundance, Beauty, Prosperity, Purity

Ganesha (Hindu Masculine Deity)- Overcoming Obstacles, Success, Wealth, Good Fortune by Removing Obstacles

Shiva (Hindu Masculine Deity)- "The Destroyer", Dissolve Karma, Death and Rebirth, Transformation, Divine Masculine Energy

Vishnu (Hindu Masculine Deity)- "The Preserver", Transcend Disorder into Peace, Transformation

Krishna (Hindu Masculine Deity)- Love and Compassion, Enlightenment, Soul's Journey, Transcending Ego

Durga (Hindu Feminine Deity)- Light Against Darkness, Divine Power to Eliminate Negative Energy, Feminine Power

Kali (Hindu Feminine Deity)- Shadow Work, Understanding and Transmuting Personal Demons

Saraswati (Hindu Feminine Deity)- Intuition, Creation, Art and Music, Greater Wisdom, Expression

Oshun (Orisha of Yoruba Religion)- Water, Divine Feminine, Love, Beauty, Abundance, Confidence, Feminine Power and Sensuality
Kuan Yin (Buddhism)- Mercy, Compassion, Love, Open Heart Chakra, Gentle Protection, Healing

Green Tara (Tibetan Buddhism)- Gentle Heart Healing, Forgiveness, Serenity, Allowing, Comfort

Venus (Roman Goddess)- Goddess of Love, Relationship Healing, Self Love, Beauty, Prosperity, Fertility

Brigid (Celtic Goddess)- Protection, Clarity, Direction, Confidence, Life Purpose, Sacred Healing

Isis (Ancient Egyptian Goddess)- Healing, Awaken Healing Gifts, Magic, Protection, Invoking Personal Power

Hecate (Ancient Greek Goddess)- Shadow Work, Magic, Witchcraft, Uncover Subconscious Blocks, Spirit World

Part Two:
Spells, Incantations, and Activations

Introduction

In this section, you will find 33 different 'spells' broken up by category. The word spell is simply a term used to describe words that hold magic. All words hold an element of power within them. It is no coincidence that the root of the word spelling is 'spell'. Over time, the word 'spell' has been associated with negativity, exacerbated by historical persecution, literature, and even Hollywood demonizing those who understand how to harness the power available to us all. Anything you speak, think, and write can be a spell if you put the power of your energy behind it.

Every spell in this book has been channeled and infused with energy. You will notice each spell varies in length and format; this is because all were channeled to give the most power to the individual intention held within the spell. Speak the words slowly and from the heart. Your energy will magnify the energy already infused in each word.
Every spell in this book is protected and protective. You will not be able to harm yourself or others using the words written here. You may find that after you state a particular spell, events unfold or energy shifts within your life. Some might mistake this as negative, but any manifestation of a spell is an unfoldment of your intentions. Sometimes things need to shift to create the desired outcome. Trust the process as you travel through the incredible journey of your self-healing, growth, awakening, and personal magic.

Your faith and trust will be the propelling force as the magic unfolds in your life. We can sabotage ourselves with doubt and fear. We can state an incantation and immediately squash it with our energy. State each word with belief and knowing the magic begins to unfold the moment to state it. Recognize doubt but do not feed into doubt.

As stated previously, it is recommended to do a clearing and protection ritual before stating any of the spells. This will ensure you are in the most open and Divine setting to work your magic. These can be done in only a few minutes, and are worth the time spent.

Make these spells your own. They are tools that can be combined with many other metaphysical tools, such as candles, crystals, and music. Set the space for yourself. Use this as time devoted to yourself because you deserve it.

You may instantly feel, see, or experience the effects of these incantations. Allow yourself time and space to process each incantation after it is spoken. Once you know how a spell affects you, you can feel free to use it regularly. They act as affirmations, integrating your beliefs with the magic. Stating them multiple times in a singular or separate spell sessions can help amplify their power. Some spells, however, you only need to state once and you will know its power the moment you state it. Let those integrate and manifest without multiple sessions.

How you use this book is your individual decision. Lean on your intuition and feelings to guide you. They will lead you to the best incantations, show you how to use them, and how often to use them. Trust your desires. There is no right or wrong.

This spiritual journey can be very deep but I personally encourage you to allow in lightness while you transform. Soft energy allows us more space to manifest and create, and frankly, you deserve to enjoy the journey of life.

Love and Relationship Spells

Spell 1: Attract New Relationship

I call in the energy of a new romantic relationship.
I call in the Soul of this kindred partnership.
May the most divine Soul be attracted to me,
And show themselves in Source's purity.

May we recognize each other upon meeting.
This relationship shalt not be fleeting,
But rather the perfect Divine Partner for me,
Who is ready to meet all my needs.

I call in the following for the Highest and Best Good
[List traits of the relationship you are calling in]

So be it and so it is.

Spell 2: Call in SoulMate or Twin Flame

Fellow Soul who is part mine, I summon thee.
The time has come for Unity.
May all old energies fall away.
And Divine Helpers bring you back to me.
I call in my Soul Mate now.
I drop all questions of how.
Come home sweet beloved, come home.

And so it is. Love, Gratitude and Blessings.

Spell 3: Heal Relationship

I now heal the energy between myself and [other person].
I call on both our Higher Selves to assist.
I call on all Divine Helpers, Angels, and Guides to please assist.
I ask that we both receive clarity and guidance on how to heal.
[Visualize Other Individual]

I am speaking to the Higher Self of [name].
I desire healing within our relationship.
I intend that we both come to understanding and forgiveness.
I am willing to forgive you for the following hurts
[List everything you wish to forgive them for]

I ask for forgiveness for the following
[List everything you wish to be forgiven for]

I cut all cords of past karmas that caused conflict and hurt.
I ask that we understand our life lessons,
but let go of old energy that does not serve us.

I call in Divine Healing energy to surround us both.
Heal us individually and collectively.
Let us forgive, learn, and grow.
Allow us to completely heal.
We now move away from patterns of pain into patterns of love.
We are now healed and ready to start anew.

Spell 4: Cutting Cords

[This incantation can be used to cut cords with a specific person or general cords that are known or unknown to you]

Specific Person

I call on Archangel Michael to assist, please.

I now cut all cords with [name] of pain, hurt, fear, codependency, guilt, shame, traumas, wounds, emotional or physical abuse, and neglect, unworthiness, anger, and hatred.
I cut all cords of past karmas, keeping the wisdom but releasing the negative energy.
I cut all cords that keep us in any unhealthy cycle or karmic loop.
I ask that all cords are dissolved upon their point of creation.
I ask that the wounds from these cords are healed immediately.
May all of this be done for the highest and best good for us both and our Souls' expansion.

-If you desire to cut relationship cord with an individual-
Bring the individual to mind.
Ask to speak to their Higher Self.
State that you desire to cut all cords with them.
Thank them for all they taught you and for the karma you helped one another resolve.
State 'I now cut this cord, across all lifetimes, timelines and realities, with love and forgiveness. So be it and so it is.'

General Relationship Cords

I cut all cords of past vows and commitments to past partners, in this life or past incarnations, that are not my Soul Mate or Twin Flame.
I cut all cords to karmic relationships that do not serve my highest good.
I cut all cords with limiting beliefs or energy of abandonment, heartbreak, fear of loss, shunning, hurt, non-acceptance, threats, adultery, deception, abuse, neglect, unworthiness, treachery, poverty, sacrifice, shock, fear, rage, hatred, anger, shame, undeservingness, guilt, revenge, vengeance, sickness, loss, blame, and persecution, in this lifetime or past lifetimes, across all realities and dimensions. I cut all negative ties within

myself, between myself and anyone else, and between myself and my Twin Flame or SoulMate.
So be it and so it is. It is done.

You can state this incantation on behalf of your Twin Flame or Soul Mate. Ask for the permission of their Higher Self first and state it for their highest and best good.
If you do not take these steps, the incantation will not work.

Spell 5: Improve Communication

I call upon the assistance of Archangel Gabriel to help clear all communication blocks and barriers between myself and [name of other party].

Clear, Clear, Clear all energy that blocks free, open communication with [name].
Clear, Clear, Clear all known and unknown obstacles that create barriers to communication with [name].
Clear, Clear, Clear all energy of misunderstandings, past, present, and future, between myself and [name].
Clear, Clear, Clear all karmas, subconscious patterns, or habits that lead to communication blocks and barriers between myself and [name].
Clear, Clear, Clear all fear surrounding communication with [name].

I ask Archangel Gabriel to please pull out and dissolve all energetic barriers to communication between myself and [name].
I breathe in the energy of fresh, new communication [inhale].
I breathe out all remaining, stagnant energy [exhale].
{DO THIS 3X}

I open now to new, free communication with [name].
May we talk openly, freely, and frequently.
May we listen and speak without judgment.
May we always understand each others' perspectives.
May we enjoy all conversations with one another.
May we talk with joy, fun, and much laughter.
May we both be brave enough to talk openly, starting now.

And so it is. With love, and much gratitude.

Self Healing and Empowerment

Spell 6: Release Fear and Doubt

Release, Release, Release all fear and doubt from within me.
Release, Release, Release all fear and doubt from within my mind.
Release, Release, Release all fear and doubt from within my emotions.
Release, Release, Release all fear and doubt from within my body.
Release, Release, Release all fear and doubt from my energy field.

I dissolve all fear and doubt from the source point of their very first creation.
I send this energy down through the soles of my feet into Mother Earth to recycle and transmute into neutral energy.
I call in the energy of freedom, security, and confidence to replace all fear and doubt within me.
I ask that a barrier of love forms within and around me.
And that this energy barrier instantly transmutes any future fear or doubt into Divine Knowing and trust.

Thank you Mother Earth for transmuting my pain.
I send you love and much gratitude in return.

Spell 7: Self Love and Confidence

I am worthy, whole, and complete as I am right now.
I release all karmic, subconscious, and limiting beliefs that create blocks to unconditional self-love.
I release all energy of unworthiness NOW.
I release all energy of not feeling good enough NOW.
I release all energy of insecurity NOW.
I release all energy of undeserving NOW.
I release all self-doubt and judgment NOW.

I call in and embrace the energy of pure unconditional love.
I call in and embrace the energy of self-worth.
I call in and embrace the energy of unwavering confidence.
I call in and embrace the energy of authenticity.

I love and honor who I am now and forevermore.
There is nothing to fix within me.
I relinquish and heal all false programming and conditioning that made me feel unlovable.

I know I am Divine.
I know I am Limitless.
I know I am Unique.
I am Source and Source is perfect. Therefore I know I cannot be anything less than Perfect.

I deserve love.
I deserve LOVE.
I DESERVE LOVE.

I now embody complete self-love, pure potential, and peace in every moment, from now on.

I give gratitude to the Light within me
I am one with Source, who is pure perfection.
My existence is the embodiment of this perfection.

I promise to always honor myself.
I vow to always see myself through the lens of Divine Love.

And so it is.

Spell 8: Step into Personal Power

May the fire burn from within my core,
May I feel my power more and more.
I step into my fullest expansion now,
I allow, allow, allow.
No longer will I sit around and pray,
That my power comes to me one day.
That day is now and forevermore,
Doubt and fear I no longer endure.

I accept my fullest power to create,
No longer hiding in the shadows of shame.
It is safe for me to be myself,
I stop all comparison to anyone else.

I am ready and accept the power of the Divine,
Knowing this power has always been mine.
I unlock my magic from deep within,
I embody the power given by Him.
I unleash the power ever so pure,
I embody the power given by Her.

And it is so.

Spell 9: Peace and Tranquility

I breathe in the energy of peace,
From the stillest lake.
And I embody this now.

I breathe in the energy of tranquility,
From the highest mountain top.
And I embody this now.

I breathe in the energy of unity,
From the most peaceful forest.
And I embody this now.

I breathe in the energy of calmness,
From the summer night sky.
And I embody this now.

I breathe in the energy of quietness,
From the break of a new dawn.
And I embody this now.

I breathe in the energy of harmony,
From nature's perfect ecosystem.
And I embody this now.

I breathe in the energy of groundedness,
From the deepest roots in the oldest forest.
And I embody this now.

I breathe in all the energy of peace and tranquility,
From earth and heaven's infinite flow.
And I embody this now and forever.

And so it is. Thank you.

Spell 10: Physical or Mental Healing

--You may also say this on behalf of a loved one, for their highest and best good.--

I call on all Divine Helpers, Guides, and Archangel Raphael to please assist in my healing. Thank you all. I give you my love and gratitude in exchange for your assistance.

I call in now the most powerful, healing light of the Divine I can handle safely at this time.
I ask this energy surrounds all areas within me that need to be healed.
[You may call it to specific areas now].

I instruct this beautiful Divine Healing Light to heal all areas of imbalance and dis-ease upon the point of their very first creation.
I instruct this Divine Healing Light to expand throughout my entire being, making whole all parts within me.
I instruct this Divine Healing Light to infuse every part of my mental, emotional, physical, and energetic being, creating complete harmony within me.
I instruct this Divine Healing Light to bring me back to full physical, mental, emotional, and spiritual health and wellness now.

I open now to the guidance and wisdom this dis-ease is telling me.
I take this wisdom with me and release all need for current or future imbalance now.
I release all energies that created this dis-ease now and forever.

I ask this is all done for my highest and best good and the highest and best good of all involved.

I AM HEALTHY.
I AM HEALED.
I AM WHOLE.
I AM IN PERFECT BALANCE, MIND, BODY, AND SPIRIT.

Thank you, thank you, thank you.
So be it. It is Done.

[Drink a full glass of water and rest after this incantation]

Bonus Spell: Healthy Weight or Ideal Body Type

I release all energy that creates an imbalance in my weight and body now.
I release all unhealthy ideas I have about myself and my body.
I release the need to store weight as a form of protection.
I release the underlying mental, emotional, or physical causes that create excess weight now.
I release all subconscious programs that prevent me from obtaining and maintaining my ideal weight now.

From this moment on, it is easy for me to reach my ideal body weight and shape.
I effortlessly take action that leads to the healthiest version of me now.
It is incredibly easy for me to lose all excess weight.
It is incredibly easy for me to obtain my desired body shape now.

I am worthy and deserving of easily reaching my desired body weight and shape now.
I am worthy and deserving of easily maintaining my desired body weight and shape now.

I am strong. I am healthy. I eat what is best for me and I love the food I eat. I engage in activities that are best for me, and I love the activities I engage in.

I know my body is not a reflection of my loveability and I deserve to feel confident about myself at all times. I release all guilt or shame about my body. I release all guilt or shame about wanting to lose weight or having a particular body type. I accept my desires and honor myself.

I was given the power as a Divine Creator to choose how I want my physical appearance to look. I embody the power now to shift my body in the ways that I desire. I honor my body. I love my body. I enjoy my physical appearance.

I set the intentions for my body now and they begin to manifest immediately upon me declaring them.

[State now your intentions and/or visualize your desired result.]

So be it and so it is. Thank you.

Bonus Spell: Anti-Aging or Reverse Aging Spell

I state the following incantation for my highest good, in accordance with the Divine Plan of my Soul.

I call upon the energy of youth which is available to us all.
May this energy enter my mind and body now.
This energy repairs all that has been impacted by aging.
This energy returns all to its youthful form.

I am a Divine Being who is ageless, and I now reflect this ageless energy in my mind and body.
I release all limiting beliefs around aging.
I release the belief that we must age.
I allow the energy of youth to infuse my skin now.
I allow the energy of youth to infuse my body now.
I allow the energy of youth to infuse my mind now.

My skin is forever tight, firm, and glowing.
My bodily cells vibrate with the energy of vitality and health.
My mind, memory, and cognitive processes are forever sharp, clear, and functioning at an optimal level.

I release my need to age.
I release my need for illness or ailments.
I allow the energy of the fountain of youth to flow over me and through me.

As I state my following intentions, I declare the manifestations of these intentions are grounded immediately into my mind, body, and energy.

[State your intentions now.]

So be it and so it is. I give thanks.

Unlock Magic Within

Spell 11: Unlock Unique Gifts Spell

I open now to the full unleashing
Of the most sacred teaching.
The teachings of my Soul,
For these I always Know.

I unlock my innate gifts,
And all the energetic shifts
That will allow my truest potential
Grounding in the existential.

From the shadows to the light
My Highest Self takes flight.
From darkness to clarity,
Understanding all polarity.

I am ready and declare,
With true conviction and care,
My powers and gifts now appear
Without any doubt or fear.

With these words I now invoke,
The power of my protective cloak,
Making it safe for me to awaken
All magic that lies within.

I fully embody and embrace
Across all time and space
My gifts, magic, and power,
May they blossom as the flower.

It is done. For the highest and best good. Thank you, thank you, thank you.

Spell 12: Violet Flame Invocation Spell

I call upon the Violet Flame now.
And I ask assistance from Saint Germain and all Divine helpers of alchemy.
I ask this Violet Flame surrounds myself and my space,
Clearing, cleansing, and transmuting all low vibrational energy into pure love and light.

I ask the Violet Flame alchemizes all
Hate into love
Pain into healing
Lack into abundance
Unease into balance
Confusion into clarity
Darkness into light
Anxiety into peace
Doubt into trust
Fear into knowing
Failure into success
Conflict into resolution
Indecision into intuition
Restriction into freedom
Reluctance into bravery
Powerlessness into empowerment
Stagnation into action
Withholding into expression
Ego into Divinity
Blockages into flow.

I call the Violet Flame into the following relationships or areas of my life [state where you desire to use this]. Transmuting all old energy into fresh loving, joyful, and abundant energy now. [State all specific energies you wish to transmute, and how you would like to transmute them. Example. Transmute debt into prosperity].

Thank you, Saint Germain and the beautiful Violet Flame for assisting me today. With much love and gratitude, so be it and so it is.

Spell 13: Uncover Life Purpose Spell

I call upon my Higher Self, guides, angels, and Divine helpers to assist in the uncovering of my purpose, Soul contracts, and Divine mission both during this lifetime and at this very moment.

I am open to know my role on earth as part of the Divine.

I ask that my intuition is opened and I am able to clearly distinguish between Divine Guidance and ego or conditioning.

I ask to be shown signs, synchronicities, and directions to lead me to my Highest Divine Path in all moments.

I ask to be aligned now, mentally, emotionally, physically, energetically, and materially to my life purpose.

I ask for Divine empowerment to help me create and manifest my desires in the physical.

I relinquish all blocks to the fullest realization of my Divine Life Purpose and I ask Divine energy to please dissolve and remove all obstacles from my path now.

So be it and so it is. Thank you.

Spell 14: Spiritual Downloads Spell

I ask now that sacred knowledge from ancestors and helpers Divine
Be downloaded and embedded into my mind.
Please show me what I am ready to know
Gratitude I give for these gifts bestowed.

I open my mind, body, and soul
To knowledge from the sacred scroll.
I allow new spiritual downloads in
Transforming what has been
Into new expansive energy
Merging in complete synergy.

I ask this process is gentle and kind
In my physical and my mind.
I ask to easily embody the new
In what I think, say, and do.

Please allow the download integration now.
Show me all…who, what, where, and how.
I am open, open, open to receive.
A new tapestry these energies weave.
Show me the way through signs and synchronicity,
I follow your guidance, my Divine committee.

Thank you, thank you, thank you. It is done.

Spell 15: Connect with Angels or Spirit Guides

I call upon my guides, angels, and any other light beings who are assisting me at this time.
I ask to please be shown now who you are, your origin, and your names.
I ask to please be shown signs of your presence and guidance in my life.
I am open to this revelation now, and in the days to come.

Thank you from the bottom of my heart for all of your Divine assistance in my journey.
I am ready to know and work with you on a more personal level now.
I am ready to ascend to the next stage of my journey with your assistance.
Please show me what I am ready to know.
I ask you to please reveal yourself.
Thank you, thank you, thank you.

[Please go into silent meditation and journal all intuitions you get. This is something that may all be revealed at once or over the course of time. It is advised you keep a record of what you get.]

Success and Abundance Spells

Spell 16: Money Spell

I now clear all blocks to abundance, prosperity, and financial wealth now.
I dissolve all cords and past vows of poverty from this lifetime or previous lifetimes.
I dissolve all limiting beliefs about money from this lifetime or past lifetimes.
I release and heal all karmic and ancestral consciousness of lack and blocks to money.
I release all energy of lack from my mind, emotions, body, spirit, and akasha now.
I let go, release, and dissolve anything within me, conscious or unconscious, that is holding me back from abundance in any way. NOW.

I open myself up to receive unlimited abundance from known and unknown sources now.
I open myself up to receive large sums of money and consistent income now.
I am open and receptive to receive all forms of abundance, prosperity, and financial wealth at this moment and each moment moving forward.

I release all habits around money that do not serve my abundance.
I now call in the Spirit of money.
I allow this energy to merge with my being now.

I feel my Oneness with the Energy of the Universe.
I feel my worthiness to receive money and abundance in all forms.
I feel my deservingness of abundance, security, and financial freedom.

I call in the most powerful energy of abundance that I can handle at this moment.
I set the intention this energy of abundance continues to flow to me from this moment forward.

I release all worries and fear about money to the Divine now and ask they are instantly transmuted into the energy of abundance.
From this moment forward, I am an abundant being.
I am prosperous.
I am wealthy.
Money flows to me easily and effortlessly.

I ask that any lessons surrounding money be gently shown to me now and I release the energy within me that has created any and all lack in my life.

Everything I do leads to more and more abundance.
I honor myself and everyone else in this process.
I heal all wounds that led to lack in my life.
I fully open to and embrace a life of pure abundance now and forever.

I ground this energy into myself and my world now. Money is attracted to me and I now decide how much money I call in. I own my power to create my reality and I attract unlimited amounts of money into my life. From this moment forward, I have all of the money I need to pay for everything I need, want, and desire.

So be it and so it is. Thank you Spirit of money, Thank you, Divine.

Spell 17: Manifestation Spell

With the words I speak now, I create the reality I desire.
I know I create my reality.
I know I have the power of the Divine.
I step into my power now.
I release all ego programming, limiting beliefs, and self-sabotage from my mind, emotions, body, and spirit now.
I use my Divine Power to create the circumstances and experiences I desire for my highest and best good and the highest and best good of all.

I manifest the following now
[State out loud or visualize all that you intend to manifest.]

I am worthy of these manifestations.
I am deserving of these manifestations.

I call all of these or greater into my reality now.
I ground in this energy and see it begin to manifest instantly.

I call in my Higher Self, Guides and Angels to help lead my actions, thoughts, and words to create this reality or better now.

I surrender these to the Divine and know they are manifesting now for my highest and best good.

So be it and so it is. Thank you.

Spell 18: Success Spell

I am open and ready for success in my life.
I release all blocks I hold consciously, unconsciously, or karmically to success.
It is safe for me to be successful now.
Others are supportive of my success.
I release all fears I have about success.
I release all potential sabotaging energy to my success.

The time has come, the time has come.
No longer will I hide in the shadows.
No longer will I play it small.
No longer will I hold myself back.

I am perfect, whole, and complete.
I deserve success.
I own my power and potential.
I allow myself to grow more and more into my limitless potential as a Divine Creator.

I am here for a reason and at this moment, I fully step into my Soul's calling.
I experience success in everything I do.
I allow the Universe and others to support me in this success.
I call success into every area of my life now.
I fully embody the energy of success in every area of my life now.

So be it and so it is. Thank you.

Spell 19: Clear All Financial Blocks

I clear all financial blocks now.
I clear all financial blocks I hold within my mind now.
I clear all financial blocks I hold within my beliefs now.
I clear all financial blocks I hold within my emotions now.
I clear all financial blocks I hold within my body now.
I clear all financial blocks I hold within my energy field now.
I clear all financial blocks I hold from any past incarnations now.
I clear all financial blocks I hold within any alternate realities or timelines now.
I clear all financial blocks I hold from my ancestry now.
I clear all financial blocks I hold due to fear now.
I clear all financial blocks I took on from either of my parents now.
I clear all financial blocks I hold due to feelings of unworthiness now.

My energy field is now entirely and completely free from all financial blocks now and forever.
I create a protective field around me that prevents any financial blocks from forming or entering my energy.
I call in the energy of abundance, wealth, financial security, prosperity, gratitude, and freedom now.
[Speak the next statement even stronger]
I call in the energy of abundance, wealth, financial security, prosperity, gratitude, and freedom now.
[Speak it now with all your energy]
I call in the energy of abundance, wealth, financial security, prosperity, gratitude, and freedom now.
I allow this energy to merge with my energy field, and I am now a being of pure abundance.
From this moment forward I attract unlimited abundance easily and effortlessly into my life.

And so it is. Thank you.

Spell 20: Career or Business Spell

I let go of all energy that created unhappy, unsuccessful, or unprofitable business or work experiences in my life.
As I let this go, I open myself up to the perfect career or business opportunities to present themselves to me.

May my career or business be blessed now with passion, prosperity, freedom, joy, peace, fulfillment, and all other energy my Soul yearns for.
I call on all Divine Beings to please assist in this process.
I align my energy now with the perfect career or business for me. This energy continues to guide and bless me with limitless opportunities to live the life I desire and deserve.

I call on a business or career with the following energies into my reality now
[List all traits you desire in your business or career].

I ask that I continue to align with these energies and I only attract opportunities that provide these energies or better into my life.
I release all expectations of failure, struggle, or fear that this is not possible to create.
I express my gratitude for the manifestation of this perfect business or career and I let it go into the arms of the Universe.

So be it and so it is. Thank you.

Releasing Spells

Spell 21: Release Old Attachments

I release all attachments, known and unknown, that no longer serve my Soul's growth. As I release these attachments, I open myself to the fresh, new energy of love, peace, abundance, security, purpose, purity, confidence, and joy.

I release the following attachments I have surrounding career, success, and money now.
[List all energy you wish to release.]

I now dissolve all known and unknown attachments that do not serve me, upon the point of their very first creation, across all lifetimes, timelines, and realities, now and forever. And so it is.

I release the following attachments I have surrounding love and relationships now.
[List all energy you wish to release.]

I now dissolve all known and unknown attachments that do not serve me, upon the point of their very first creation, across all lifetimes, timelines, and realities, now and forever. And so it is.

I release the following attachments I have surrounding self-love, worthiness, and deserving now.
[List all energy you wish to release.]

I now dissolve all known and unknown attachments that do not serve me, upon the point of their very first creation, across all lifetimes, timelines, and realities, now and forever. And so it is.

I release the following attachments I have surrounding mental or physical health now.
[List all energy you wish to release.]

I now dissolve all known and unknown attachments that do not serve me, upon the point of their very first creation, across all lifetimes, timelines, and realities, now and forever. And so it is.

I release the following attachments I have surrounding unhealthy or detrimental habits now.
[List all energy you wish to release.]

I now dissolve all known and unknown attachments that do not serve me, upon the point of their very first creation, across all lifetimes, timelines, and realities, now and forever. And so it is.

I release the following unhealthy attachments I have to other people now.
[List all energy you wish to release with other people.]

I now dissolve all known and unknown attachments that do not serve me, upon the point of their very first creation, across all lifetimes, timelines, and realities, now and forever. And so it is.

I release the following attachments I have surrounding all other energy that does not serve me now.
[List all energy you wish to release.]

I now dissolve all known and unknown attachments that do not serve me, upon the point of their very first creation, across all lifetimes, timelines, and realities, now and forever. And so it is.

Spell 22: Dissolve Blocks

I command all blocks to the life I desire to dissolve completely.
I dissolve all energy blocks that prevent living freely.
I call on the light of the Divine,
To dissolve blocks to what is rightfully mine.
All blocks to a peaceful life and mind,
All blocks to true love of any kind.

Love, freedom, joy, and peace flow into me now.
Abundance, success, and fulfillment flow into me now.
All blocks to these dissolve immediately now.
I allow, I allow, I allow, I allow.

And so it is.

Spell 23: Forgiveness Spell

[Call in who you wish to forgive and state their name]
I call the deepest energy of healing into us now.

Divine,
Help me forgive on the deepest level of my Soul.
Help me release all energy of resentment, anger, hurt, fear, guilt, shame, and sadness from my energy field now.
Heal the wounds this relationship created.
Help me understand the role this played in my life.

[State their name], I forgive you for the following [state what you wish to forgive].
With this forgiveness, I intend to let go of all past hurtful energy between us.

[State name], I ask that you please forgive me for all intentional or unintentional hurt I caused you. [If you have anything you wish to ask forgiveness for, state it here].

I intend that we both move forward, with the appropriate life lessons, and complete freedom from energetic wounds, cords, and attachments to unhealthy behaviors of the past.
I set the intention to move forward with you in the following way [State how you wish to move forward. This can be completely dissolving the relationship or stepping into a new beginning.]

I now leave all the energy of the past behind and open myself up to love.

With love and much gratitude, it is done.

Spell 24: Release Old Relationships

[Bring to mind the relationships, types of relationships, or specific people you wish to release]

I release now from my life,
All relationships that ended in strife,
All past karmics [1] that do not serve,
The loving energy that I deserve.

I cut ties with those who caused me harm,
Energetic Vampires, I now disarm.
With my words, I state my intent,
With no regret nor lament.

I release all the following relationships from my life now,
From this lifetime or past, I rescind any vow,
I took or promise I made.
May these now forever fade.

I release all ties, chords, attachments to the following people now, with love, for the Highest and Best Good of All.
[State all relationships you wish to dissolve].

I intend this energy lasts,
Until I state otherwise.
Let the past be the past.
I open to bright new skies.

It is done. Thank you.

[1] 'Karmics' is a word used to describe individuals with whom you have a karmic tie. The ones we release in this spell, are those who no longer serve your highest good.

Spell 25: Release All Unwanted Energy

[This section contains two spells. The first is for individual energy clearing. The second is for space clearing.]

Individual Energy Cleanse

I release all energy within me that causes any disharmony in my life.
I release all karmic energy that creates any blocks to my peace and happiness.
I release all energy that creates any dis-ease within my mind and body.
I release all energy that creates discord within my relationships.
I release all heavy energy, curses, hexes, or ill-intent from others from this lifetime, past lifetimes, other realities and timelines, NOW.
I release and heal all ill-will, words, thoughts, and actions I directed towards myself or others that created disharmony in my reality or their reality, in this lifetime or past lifetimes. I ask for Divine forgiveness and healing of all these energies now.
I ask to be gently shown any life lessons I need to learn and release all harmful energy surrounding them now.
I call in the highest vibration healing energy to completely clear my energy field, mind, body, akashic records, and emotions of any low vibration energy now.
I call in the highest vibration healing energy to clear all of my chakras and meridians of blockages or vritis [1].
I clear myself now of all negative energetic cycles. I ask the underlying energy is dissolved now and I move forward with wisdom, ease, and grace.
I release and dissolve all negative, harmful, or chaotic energy I have or am still creating with any other person in my life. I call in the energy of love, healing, peace, and harmony into our unified energy field now.
It is done, it is done, it is done, thank you.

[1] Vriti is the Sanskrit word for whirlpool. Often describing energetic whirlpools held in our Chakra System.

Space Clearing

I call upon the highest vibration Divine healing energy into my home, work, and any other space I reside in. I ask that this beautiful Divine energy locates, heals, and transmutes all negative and low vibration energy from these spaces now. I ask that the energy is instantly alchemized into freedom, love, peace, and beauty. I call on the Divine Energy to locate all underlying causes of low vibration energies within my space and heal them at the root level now. I ask that any and all beings who are not of love, light, or hold my best interest in their heart, leave my space now. I ask a team of angels to please escort all lower vibrational beings or entities from this space and prevent them from coming back. I ask that these angels please continue to protect my loved ones, my space, and myself from any and all low vibration energy moving forward. I ask that a protective shield is placed around my living space to ward off all lower vibration energies from entering or staying in the space. I ask that all lower vibration energies are instantly transmuted into Divine peace upon entering my space.

Thank you, thank you, thank you. So be it. It is done, it is done, it is done.

Spiritual Expansion Spells

Spell 26: Heart Opening Spell

May all walls around my heart crumble and fall,
May all energy of pain dissolve.
I am safe to be vulnerable and love.
I call on Divine Energy from above.

I open my heart to receive love from all,
May all other beings hear this call.
To love and be loved is the greatest gift of all.

My heart is open to give and receive freely,
As I now experience love more fully.
Divine love expands through my chest,
And radiates out to touch all the rest.

With love, it is done. Thank you.

Spell 27: Chakra Balancing Spell

<u>First Chakra</u>
Focus attention at the base of the spine- Root Chakra
Chant 'LAM'

State:
I now release all fear, doubt, financial blocks, and insecurities.
I call in grounding energy of abundance, stability, and authenticity.

My root chakra is now clear, open, and balanced.

<u>Second Chakra</u>
Focus attention below belly button- Sacral Chakra
Chant 'VAM'

State:
I now release all emotional, creative, and sexual blockages.
I call in the flowing energy of childhood healing, flexibility, creativity, and intimacy.

My sacral chakra is now clear, open, and balanced.

<u>Third Chakra</u>
Focus attention above the belly button- Solar Plexus Chakra
Chant 'RAM'

State:
I now release all confidence blocks, unworthiness, and limiting ego patterns.
I call in the fire energy of deservingness, confidence, and Divine action.

My solar plexus chakra is now clear, open, and balanced.

Fourth Chakra
Focus attention on the center of the chest- Heart Chakra
Chant 'YAM'

State:
I now release all blocks to giving or receiving unconditional love.
I call in the air energy of self-love and heart-centered connection with others.

My heart chakra is now clear, open, and balanced.

Fifth Chakra
Focus attention on throat- Throat Chakra
Chant 'HAM'

State:
I now release all communication blocks.
I call in the energy of the Ethers to speak my truth, have balanced communication, and mutual understanding at all times.

My throat chakra is now clear, open, and balanced.

Sixth Chakra
Focus attention on the area between eyebrows- Third Eye Chakra
Chant 'OM'

State:
I now release all deceptive thinking patterns and blocks to my intuition.
I call in Divine energy of intuition, higher knowing, and Divine Truth.

My third eye chakra is now clear, open, and balanced.

Seventh Chakra

Focus attention on the crown of the head- Crown Chakra
Chant 'AH

State:
I now release all human conditioning, old programs, limiting beliefs, and feelings of separation.
I call in Divine Energy to align me with Source always and forever.

My crown chakra is now clear, open, and balanced.

Spell 28: Align with Source Spell

Source, God, Creator I call on thee,
Open me up to your Divine Grace.
Let me embody your energy fully,
And share your love with the human race.

Flow through my mind, emotions, and body,
Flow through my thoughts, words, and actions.
Let me be a clear channel for your energy.
Let me feel my Oneness with all that is.

Thank you, thank you, thank you. Om, Shanti, Amen. [1]

[1] Om is the mantra of the Divine. Shanti is Sanskrit for peace. Amen means 'so be it'.

Spell 29: Transcend Ego Spell

My dear ego,
I thank you for keeping me safe,
I thank you for navigating my way.
The time has come for us to become One,
And for you to merge with the larger sum,
Of who I am, which is Source,
And let the Divine lead my course.

From this moment on I listen only to God,
Who gives to me a perspective so broad.
May all the ego cords be cut free,
As my mind and actions align with THEE.

So be it and so it is. Thank you.

Spell 30: Open Third Eye Intuition Spell

Open, Open, Open my sacred third eye.
Open, Open, Open my channel to Source.
Open, Open, Open my energy flow.
Open, Open, Open my ability to know.
May I hear my Higher Guidance loud and clear,
May I always distinguish between truth and fear.
I open now to perpetual guidance from above,
And vow to live in sacred love.

I am now open and receptive to continuous, intuitive guidance. For my highest and best good and the highest and best good of all.
Thank you.

Advanced Spells

Spell 31: Attunement Spell

It is recommended you meditate for 10 or more minutes after stating the following incantation.

I call upon Divine forces to aid in my attunement process.
I call upon the protection and assistance of Angels, Gods and Goddesses, and Ascended Masters during my attunement.
I ask that I am attuned now to God, my Higher Self, and healing energies.
I ask that I am attuned to my natural powers.
I ask that I am attuned to channel Source energy.
I open my crown chakra and allow the Divine Energy in.
I ask this energy flows through each one of my chakras, opening and aligning each with the Divine.
I vow to only use this Divine connection and gift for the highest and best good of all.
So be it and so it is.
Thank you, thank you, thank you.

Now lie down and allow the attunement to integrate.

Spell 32: Ancestral Healing Spell

I call upon Divine Source energy, my personal guides and angels, and all other light beings who can assist in the healing of my ancestral lineage now.

I ask the highest vibrational Divine healing energy flow through the entire lineage on both my mother and father's sides.

I ask this Divine energy to please heal, clear, and dissolve all wounds, karmas, blocks, and traumas carried within my lineage. Please heal and dissolve these upon the point of their very first creation.

I call in all Souls in my Soul Tribe and ancestral line now. And ask Divine Light to please surround and embrace each Soul.

I ask this Divine Light expands across all lifetimes, timelines, and realities now, healing, clearing, and returning to balance all Souls of lower vibrational energy now.

I ask that this Divine Energy returns all Souls their true Divinity, and restores health, peace, love, abundance, bliss, and joy to all.

I ask this Divine Energy clear a pathway of healing for all generations moving forward across all time and space. And that all Souls born into this lineage are returned to their crystalline energy upon incarnation.

May we keep the wisdom gained through lifetimes and release the harsh energy absorbed through our life lessons.

May we continue to learn, grow, and evolve as our Souls desire, from a clear energetic state.

I ask this for the highest and best good of all involved.

So mote it be. Thank you.

Spell 33: Open Akashic Records Spell

Instructions

State opening incantation.
Meditate for 10-90 minutes.
State closing incantation.

Opening Meditation

I call upon the guardians of the akashic records now.
Please come forth to assist in my journey today.
I ask that you please bring forth the records that will benefit me the most at this time.
Please help guide me during my meditation and show me what I need to see.
I give my permission to open my akashic records now.
Open, open, open.
I am safe and ready to receive what I need from my akashic records now.
I set aside my ego, mental body, limiting beliefs, and all other potential barriers to this knowledge being received and understood accurately.
I ask that the record is opened and shown to me now that will assist in my intentions for this session [state any intentions now].
My akashic records are now open and remain open until I close them.

[Go into meditation. It can help if you visualize a book being opened. Read the words, allow the pictures to unfold into different visuals, and allow yourself to follow what you are shown without doubt.]

I thank the guardians of the akashic records for assisting in this process.
I intend that all knowledge gained helps guide me in my Soul's journey.
I now close my akashic records at this time.
I give the records back to the Divine guardians for safekeeping.
I thank the Universe for all knowledge shown to me during this process.
I am open to new insights entering my conscious awareness when I am ready to receive them.
The records are closed and sealed with love and gratitude.
So be it and so it is. Thank you.

The End. The New Beginning.

Thank you for being you. May the Divine bless you in all of your words, thoughts, and actions. May you live in alignment, peace, joy, love, and abundance. I am grateful to you and honor you.

Much love,
Rachael

About the Author

Rachael, just like you, is a Soul on the journey Home. On her path, she discovered she had the ability to channel energy. She has her Masters in Clinical Counseling and Reiki and worked as a practitioner for years, doing in-person and distance coaching and healing. Recently she was guided to channel and create Divine works to share on a larger scale. This book is one of those creations, designed to give you tools for self-healing and personal mastery.

Every word written in this book was Divinely channeled and infused with Energy by Rachael. She intends you feel the love, passion, and transformative energy in all of her works.

'The world is changing. This is the way of a new era. Intuitions and energy will replace old programming. The old rules of our world will be replaced by alignment with Universal Laws. I know I am here to help anchor in the energies of this Shift. Every creation is for your evolution. And I am grateful to all other Souls who are also here to ground in the Light. We are in this together. We need each other. You are not alone. Thank you.'

Additional Resources: Where to Connect with Rachael

Instagram: reiki_with_rachael
YouTube: Reiki Rachael
TikTok: rachaeltenergy
Website: https://reikiwithrachael.com

Resources and Favorite Things

I offer tons of free healings and readings on YouTube. Please check it out if you are called. Below I listed some of my favorite metaphysical tools.

Best Tarot Deck for Beginners: Rider-Waite Tarot Deck

Favorite Oracle Decks
Work Your Light Oracle
The Quantum Oracle
The Souls Journey Lesson Cards
Angel Prayers Oracle
Lemurian Starchild Oracle

Favorite Books
Autobiography of a Yogi
The Four Agreements
Mastery of Love
Animal Speak
Celestine Prophecy [Also highly recommend the movie]

Printed in Great Britain
by Amazon